EXPLORERS

OF THE

REMOTEST PLACES

ON EARTH

by Nel Yomtov

CAPSTONE PRESS
a capstone imprint

Capstone Captivate is published by Capstone Press, an imprint of Capstone.
1710 Roe Crest Drive
North Mankato, Minnesota 56003
www.capstonepub.com

**Library of Congress Cataloging-in-Publication Data is available
on the Library of Congress website.**
ISBN: 978-1-4966-8368-7 (library binding)
ISBN: 978-1-4966-8419-6 (eBook PDF)

Summary: Find out about the brave explorers who travel to the most remote
places in the world, pushing through vast forests, icy polar regions, and other
landscapes.

Image Credits
Alamy: PA Images, 8; Ceibal-Petexbatun Archaeological Project: 15; Getty
Images: Lucas Schifres, 10, Patrick AVENTURIER, 17, Sam Barker/Contour,
20, The Asahi Shimbun, 19 bottom, ullstein bild, 13; Science Source:
HOA-QUI, 19 top; Shutterstock Premier: Ryan Deboodt/Solent News, 27;
Shutterstock: AridOcean, 23, Christopher Moswitzer, Cover, 1, Gail Johnson,
22, hyunwoong park, 5 bottom, 25, kid315, 28, My Good Images, 5 top,
PeteVch, 21, rweisswald, 7, 11; Wikimedia: Kmusser, 9

Editorial Credits
Editor: Anna Butzer; Designer: Kayla Rossow; Media Researcher:
Tracy Cummins; Production Specialist: Katy LaVigne

Printed and bound in the USA.
PA117

TABLE OF CONTENTS

Words in **bold** are in the glossary.

WHERE FEW HAVE GONE

For some people, the need to explore runs deep. They take exploration to extreme levels. Over thousands of years, people have mastered the seas and discovered new lands. They have flown into space. Why do people explore in dangerous and unknown places? Curiosity is one reason. They simply want to know what's out there. Many explorers are also driven by the thrill of adventure or challenging nature's extreme settings.

Some explorers journey to **remote** places on the planet. They risk their safety in search of scientific discovery, adventure, and the desire to know. Follow these extreme explorers who have gone where few others have.

A remote jungle in Bali, Indonesia

Hang Son Doong, a remote cave in Vietnam

Chapter 1
CHARLES BLACKMORE

The Taklamakan Desert in Central Asia is one of the harshest places on Earth. Summer temperatures reach higher than 100 degrees Fahrenheit (38 degrees Celsius). Winter temperatures drop as low as -4°F (-20°C). Very little rain falls in the desert, so there is a severe lack of water. Plant and animal life is limited.

Local people call the Taklamakan the Desert of Death. Powerful winds cause fierce dust storms that can blind travelers. Some storms whip up dust as high as 13,000 feet (4,000 meters) into the air.

The Taklamakan Desert is one of the world's largest sandy deserts.

Blackmore (front left) and his team
were called the Royal Green Jackets.

No one had ever crossed the entire length of the Taklamakan. But in 1993, English explorer Charles Blackmore and a team of assistants successfully crossed the Desert of Death. They brought 30 camels with them. The group went straight into the heart of the desert where no one had ever gone. One of the **expedition**'s goals was to raise money for a children's cancer fund in England.

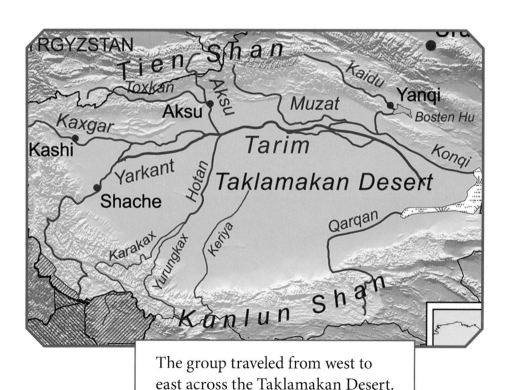

The group traveled from west to east across the Taklamakan Desert.

Blackmore and his group crossed 780 miles (1,400 kilometers) in 59 days. The **trek** across the Taklamakan was filled with danger and hardship. Traveling across miles of 1,000-foot (305-m) sand hills was painfully slow. Many group members became sick with a disease of the **intestines** caused by infection. Several members almost died from the disease. Even Blackmore, a former soldier in the British Army, was unprepared for the difficult and risky journey.

It was tiring work for Blackmore and his team to tug camels over the desert hills.

Blackmore's group had done the nearly impossible. After the successful crossing, England's Queen Elizabeth sent the team a note of congratulations. The Chinese government even issued a special postage stamp in their honor.

FACT

The Taklamakan Desert is also called the Desert of No Return. According to ancient Chinese stories, evil spirits guard a great treasure that is buried in the sands.

Chapter 2

TAKESHI INOMATA

Ceibal is an ancient site tucked away in the dense rain forests of northern Guatemala in Central America. The Olmec people were the earliest inhabitants of Ceibal. Then the Mayans occupied the region until about AD 950. Today, the remote site of Ceibal is the focus of high-tech exploration.

Takeshi Inomata is a professor of anthropology at the University of Arizona. Inomata uses laser technology to make maps that reveal hidden ancient Maya architecture. An airplane equipped with powerful lasers is flown over the tall trees of the jungle. As the plane soars overhead, lasers pick out shapes on the ground below. The lasers produce maps that show the size and location of ancient structures.

Inomata and his team used a laser called LiDAR to locate Mayan structures similar to this stone carving.

One laser map produced in 2018 covered 181 square miles (470 square kilometers). Previously, maps done on foot covered less than 3.5 square miles (9 sq km) of Ceibal. Inomata's new map revealed the location of more than 15,000 ancient Maya architectural remains. They included pyramids, roads, platforms, and buildings.

Inomata and his team used the map to dig below the earth's surface to uncover and study the structures. He began digging at Ceibal in 2005 with his wife, Daniela Triadan, an anthropologist. The couple studied ancient Maya structures and artifacts to learn how Maya culture began and developed in Central America.

Inomata and his team have been digging in Ceibal for more than 10 years.

Chapter 3
THOR THORDARSON

Thor Thordarson was born in Iceland. The country is home to about 130 active and inactive volcanoes. Iceland is called the Land of Fire. It is a place where cold arctic weather exists side by side with the fiery heat of the earth. Thordarson witnessed his first volcanic **eruption** at age 6. In later years, he visited other eruptions to get a close-up look of their glowing **lava** flows.

Thordarson decided to make a career of studying volcanoes. He has studied volcanoes and volcanic rock on every continent except Africa. On June 17, 1996, he was working in New Zealand, an island off the coast of Australia. Suddenly, Mount Ruapehu erupted.

Mount Ruapehu is the largest active volcano in New Zealand.

FACT

The Māori are the native people of New Zealand. *Ruapehu* is the Māori word for "pit of noise" or "exploding pit." The volcano began erupting at least 250,000 years ago.

Thordarson jumped into a waiting helicopter and headed toward the mountain. The helicopter circled Ruapehu's crater at more than 10,000 feet (3,048 m). All Thordarson could see was a column of white steam. He began to think the eruption was a false alarm. Suddenly, Ruapehu erupted in full fury. First, it violently spewed out a column of thick, black smoke that rose 2.5 miles (4 km) high. Then the inside of the volcano lit up with flashes of crackling light. Huge blocks of rock were hurled hundreds of feet into the air. **Molten** lava oozed from cracks in the mountain. Thordarson was witnessing the beginning of a major eruption.

》》A Deadly Eruption

Exploring volcanoes is dangerous. In June 1991, scientists Katia and Maurice Krafft were filming eruptions on Mount Unzen in Japan. Without warning, they were caught in a sudden, fast-moving mass of hot ash and lava. The Kraffts were killed in the tragedy.

Maurice and Katia Krafft at Piton de la Fournaise, one of the most active volcanoes on Earth

Forty-three people died when Mount Unzen erupted in 1991.

Chapter 4
LAURA BINGHAM

Laura Bingham was born and raised in the English countryside. She left home at age 18 to travel and explore other parts of the world. In January 2016, the bold adventuress traveled across South America from west coast to east coast on a bicycle. Bingham cycled 4,350 miles (7,000 km) over 164 days from the coast of Ecuador to the coast of Argentina.

At various times during her journey, Bingham cycled with other people. She carried few supplies. She relied on the kindness of strangers for food and shelter. Bingham's biggest physical challenge was crossing the Andes Mountains. Heavy rainfall turned the mountain roads and passes into winding pits of mud. Cycling became painfully difficult and tiring.

The Andes Mountains

The Essequibo River

In 2018, Bingham led the first-ever expedition to the source of the Essequibo River in Guyana, a country in South America. Bingham traveled with two fellow explorers, Ness Knight and Pip Stewart. The journey lasted 72 days and covered 630 miles (1,014 km). The women reached the river's source in the Acarai Mountains. Then the team **kayaked** the river to where it empties in the Atlantic Ocean.

Bingham and her friends passed through dense rain forests and grasslands. They encountered dangerous animals, including poisonous snakes and jaguars. The women had to guide the kayaks down steep, plunging waterfalls and fast-moving waters. Bingham photographed the entire journey. She shared her travels with thousands of followers on social media.

Guyana

Essequibo River

Chapter 5

HOWARD LIMBERT

For some people, exploring a cave is a dream come true. What lies hidden in the dark? Are there strange rock formations or underground rivers to explore? Exploring caves can be fun, but it's risky. Falling rocks, river flooding, and falls are just a few of the dangers.

Howard Limbert of England is one of the world's leading explorers of caves. He has explored in Europe, Central and South America, Australia, and Southeast Asia. In 1989, Limbert received permission from the government of North Vietnam to explore caves in that country. For the next 20 years, Limbert and his British team explored there.

In 2009, Limbert was the first to explore Hang Son Doong in Vietnam. It is the largest cave in the world.

In 1990, Ho Khanh, a local Vietnam resident, found an opening to a cave. Over time, he forgot its location. Khanh spent many years trying to rediscover the cave but without any luck. Finally, in 2008 he found the mysterious opening. In 2009, he told Limbert about the opening. Khanh led him back to the cave to be explored for the first time.

Limbert and his team went into the cave. The cave would be known as Hang Son Doong. To Limbert's surprise, the cave turned out to be the largest in the world. Hang Son Doong is 3.1 miles (5 km) long, 656 feet (200 m) wide, and 492 feet (150 m) high.

Hang Son Doong also contains the longest underground river on Earth.

Limbert has explored Hang Son Doong more than 100 times.

Limbert returned to the cave in 2019 with a team of three world-famous divers. One year earlier, the three divers had rescued a youth soccer team that was trapped inside a cave in Thailand. Working with Limbert, the divers discovered an underwater tunnel. The tunnel connected Hang Son Doong with another gigantic cave. The world's largest cave was even bigger than anyone imagined!

FACT

Many plants and animals live inside Hang Son Doong. Forests of 160-foot- (50-m-) tall trees grow in the cave. Monkeys, bats, snakes, squirrels, and several kinds of fish and birds also live there.

Glossary

eruption (i-RUHPT-shuhn)—a sudden and violent ejection of lava, hot ash, and steam by a volcano

expedition (ek-spu-DISH-uhn)—a long trip made for a specific purpose, such as for exploration

intestine (in-TES-tin)—a long tube in the body extending below the stomach that digests food and absorbs liquids

kayak (KYE-ak)—to use a narrow boat with a small opening in the top in which you sit and paddle

lava (LAH-vuh)—the hot, liquid rock that pours out of a volcano

molten (MOHL-tuhn)—melted at a high temperature, usually describing rock or metal

remote (rih-MOHT)—far away or distant; secluded or isolated

trek (TREK)—a slow, difficult journey

Read More

Harbo, Christopher L. *The Explosive World of Volcanoes with Max Axiom Super Scientist.* North Mankato, MN: Capstone Press, 2019.

Huang, Nellie. *Explorers: Amazing Tales of the World's Greatest Adventures.* New York: DK Publishing, 2019.

Long, David. *Survivors: Extraordinary Tales from the Wild and Beyond.* London: Faber and Faber Limited, 2016.

Internet Sites

Conquering an Infinite Cave
https://www.nationalgeographic.com/magazine/2011/01/vietnam-cave/

Laura Bingham
https://www.laurabingham.org/

Taklamakan Desert Facts
https://www.beautifulworld.com/asia/china/taklamakan-desert/

Index